THE COURT WILL RISE

A short history of the Old Courthouse, Lifford, Co. Donegal

THE COURT WILL RISE

A short history of the Old Courthouse, Lifford, Co. Donegal

By

Billy Patton

with additional research by
Angela Mulreany

An Old Courthouse Publication

Published by L.A.T.C.H.
The Old Courthouse,
Lifford,
Co. Donegal,
Ireland

First Edition 2004

Copyright All Text Billy Patton 2004

ISBN 0-9547758-0-5

Design and Layout Philippa Collings
Printed by Betaprint Ltd. Dublin

All rights reserved. No part of this publication may be reproduced, copied or transmitted in any form or by any means, without prior permission of the publishers.

This publication has received support from the Heritage Council under the 2004 Publications Grant Scheme and from Donegal Local Development Company and the Leader Programme.

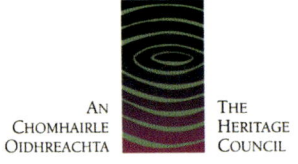

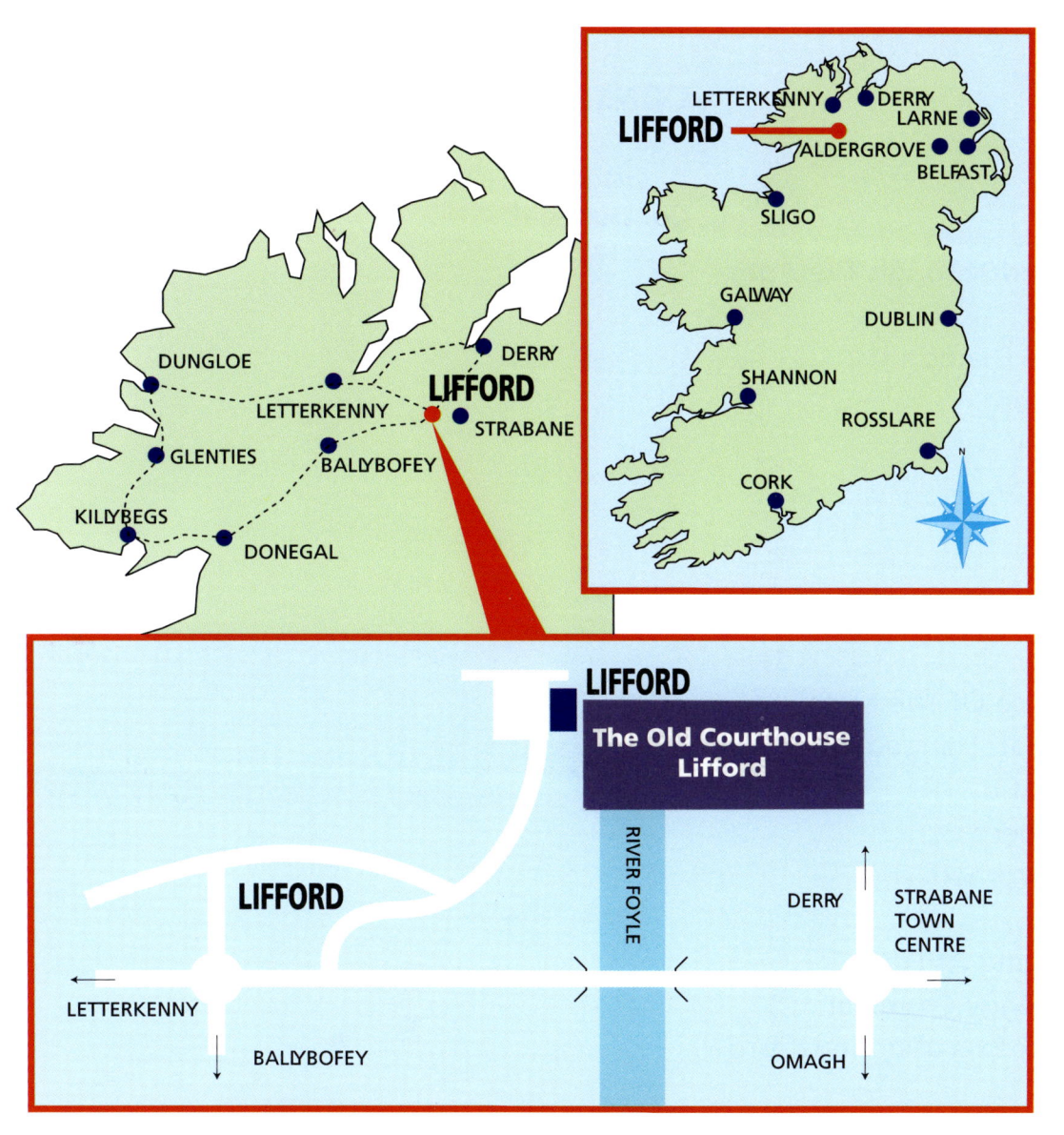

CONTENTS

Acknowledgements	8
Preface	9
Introduction - Lifford Through The Ages	10
The Courthouse	12
The Diamond In The Diamond	14
The Court Is In Session	19
Pomp And Ceremony	22
A Curious Old Custom	24
Rooms To Let	26
The County Gaol	30
The Prison Reform Act Of 1786	33
The Extreme Sentence Of The Law	
The Case Of Half-Hanged MacNaghten	36
Read All About It	38
Highway Robbery	38
The Stewart Brothers	41
Exhibit `A'	43
Another Hanging At Lifford	45
Samuel and Peggy Crummer	47
The Last Public Execution in Lifford	50

Bound For Botany Bay – 200 Years Of Transportation	54
Lifford And The Penal Colonies	56
Other Forms Of Punishment	61
The Men Of '98	
Napper Tandy	63
Captain Manus O'Donnell	65
Little Stories From The Courthouse	68
Lifford Assizes 1830	71
Pilot Charles O'Boyle	75
Legends and Escapes	
Dead or Alive?	79
Inspector Martin's Ghost	80
Footsteps in the Night	81
The Sheriff and the Sailor	83
The Lunatic Asylum	86
The Ups and Downs of Lifford Courthouse	88
Bibliography	93

ACKNOWLEDGEMENTS

The author and research team are grateful to The Heritage Council and Donegal Local Development Company for funding this publication. We are indebted to F.A.S., the Lifford Association for Tourism, Commerce and Heritage and the management of Lifford Courthouse for the time, space and facilities to undertake the project in the first place. The staff of the following libraries and archives kindly allowed us to consult and use materials in their care: Donegal County Archives; the Public Record Office Northern Ireland; County Library, Letterkenny; Lifford Branch Library; Strabane Public Library; Centre for Migration Studies, Omagh.

We are equally obliged to those who gave permission for the use of photographs and illustrations: Donegal County Archives; the Deputy Keeper of the Records, the Public Record Office of Northern Ireland for permission to reproduce a selection of photographs from the Cooper Collection (D/1422/A/1/19); Malachy McGarrigle; Michael Kennedy; The Police Museum of Belfast for the photograph featured on page 23; The Guildhall Press; Albert Johnston; Kilmainham Gaol Museum; Pauline Strain; Gerald McMenamin and Kathleen Flanagan.

Our thanks also to all those who over the years have already researched and written on the subject.

Finally, we would like to thank the enthusiastic and dedicated people who saved the Old Courthouse from deterioration. Without them all, this publication would not have been possible.

PREFACE

The Courthouse has been standing sentinel in Lifford Diamond for over 250 years. During its time as a centre for law and order it has seen years of war and peace and stirring times of upheaval and rebellion come and go. The decisions taken within its walls have affected the lives of countless men, women and children from all walks of life, often permanently and sometimes painfully.

This small book only provides a glimpse of its history and the daunting task of a comprehensive study must wait until a future date. Nevertheless, I hope you, the reader, will find something of interest in its pages and when you have finished you will at least know a little more about this fine old building and its part in Irish history.

Today the building continues to contribute to the history of law and order in Donegal. This time however, its role as a Heritage Centre is educational rather than punitive. Visitors can now safely enter the courtroom to watch re-enactments of trials and experience the atmosphere of Lifford County Gaol without the fear and trepidation experienced by the countless thousands who came before them during its long span as a working courthouse.

INTRODUCTION

LIFFORD THROUGH THE AGES

Lifford, as we know it today, did not emerge as a village until the early 1600's. Before that, the area was dominated by a series of forts and castles, the earliest and most notable being Manus O'Donnell's castle, built in 1527 to defend the strategic river crossing between Tyrone and Donegal. After the disastrous Battle of Kinsale and the eventual departure of the Gaelic chieftains in 1607, however, the stage was set for the complete take over of Ulster by the English in what became known as The Plantation.

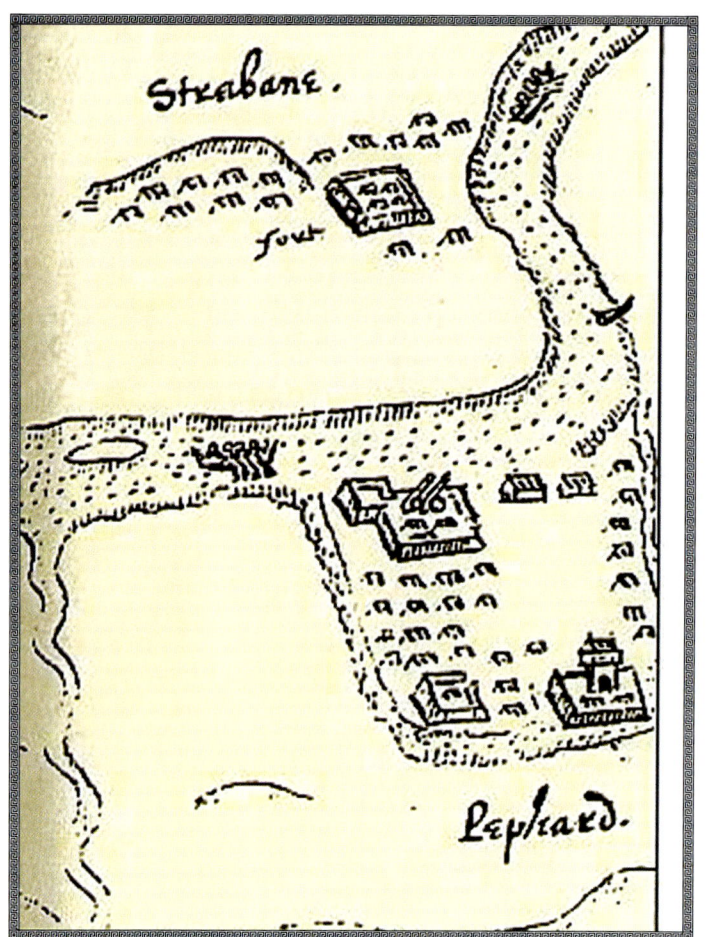

Lifford 1601

It was at this point that the Lifford area was granted to the soldier, Richard Hansard, for his services to the Crown. He commenced to settle the district with English farmers and tradesmen who built houses, cottages, a school and a church which eventually developed to form the present-day town of Lifford.

Lifford c1950

Lifford 1838

THE COURTHOUSE

By the end of the 17th century, the well-established settlers were anxious to have an administration to look after their affairs, as well as a purpose-built Courthouse which would enable a circuit assizes judge to visit the county. This became possible with the development of the Grand Jury system after 1662 which brought together the prominent landlords in the area who were bestowed with powers to raise money by means of a tax or `cess' which they levied on the county at large. The proceeds of the cess were then used for such things as the construction and repair of roads, the building and maintenance of gaols and courthouses, bringing in prisoners and, if necessary, transporting them `beyond the seas'.

It was this system, along with the required legislation, that allowed the Grand Jury to approach the architect, Michael Priestley, in 1743 to draw up plans for a Courthouse that is still regarded as *"one of the finest buildings in the North"*. The building also incorporated the County Gaol in the basement which was to last as a place of confinement for debtors, felons and eventually `lunatics', until a new gaol was completed next to the Courthouse in 1793. The Courthouse itself, however, continued to hold trials until 1938. This is its story.

The last County Donegal Grand Jury, March 1899.

THE DIAMOND IN THE DIAMOND

It's remarkable the number of old buildings in Donegal that we take for granted. We see them that often in our comings and goings we forget to look at them. In some cases, we don't think of these landmarks at all until they are gone.

The Old Courthouse in Lifford Diamond is a good example of this type of familiarity – a building that seems to have always been there, although it was touch and go a few years ago. Other people, with perhaps a more critical and appreciative eye to the intrinsic architectural significance of our famous buildings, take a different perspective on things. Here, for example, are just a few of the descriptions that have been bestowed on the Courthouse over the years:

"One of the oldest and finest courthouses in Ireland".

"One of the finest facades of its date anywhere in Ireland ... so richly endowed with elements of a quirky classicism".

"One of the finest buildings in the North".

First commissioned in 1743, it was built between 1746-1750 under the watchful eye of the Grand Jury and the architect, Michael Priestley. All of this is commemorated in a tablet under the Hanoverian arms of George the Second situated above the front entrance. Written in stone, it states: `This building was raised by the County of Donegal under the directions of Andrew Knox, Oliver McCausland, George Vaughan, Nathaniel Nesbitt, Francis Mansfield, trustees. Designed and executed by Michael Priestley A.D. 1746 Gilmore Fecit'.

George II Coat of Arms above the front door of the Courthouse

Lifford Courthouse c1930.

Very little is known about the Court, or Sessions House, as it was also called, during this initial period. We do not know, for example, how much it cost to build, although the money or most of it, would have been raised by a cess or tax levied by the Grand Jury on the county as a whole. (The Grand Jury was not a `jury' in the legal sense of the word. It was made up of prominent landowners in the area who controlled the administration of the county and was the forerunner of what we know today as the County Council).

What little we do know has been gleaned from the original Grand Jury Presentments (payments) book now held in the County Archives, Lifford. From these we learn that the site for the Courthouse was bought from the Rev. Thomas Burgoyne for £150 and was paid for in two instalments, April 1755 and September 1756. This price also included a site for a schoolhouse elsewhere in Lifford. The architect, Mick Priestley, also had to wait for his money when he was paid a total of £136.19.6 – the final payment being paid in March, 1755. This late payment may be accounted for by last-minute alterations to his original plans. This becomes apparent if the building is viewed from the front where an extra wing has clearly been added on the left, leaving the impression that the whole façade is `unbalanced'.

Despite his contribution to the history of Lifford and surrounding area, Mick Priestley remains a bit of a mystery. One of the trustees, Nathaniel Nesbitt, thought him "*a plain man, no great drawer of estimates, his skill lies mainly in his practice*". For the period, he is regarded as the "*one figure who stands out with an identifiable style and artistic personality*". Yet we don't even know the dates and places of his birth and death. His impact on the Lifford area, however, is undeniable and it is here that the Courthouse plays a crucial role. It is the only building in Ireland we know for certain to be Priestley's work and because "*it embodies in one façade many of the elements so characteristic of the work of the architect … it provides an essential reference which enables us to ascribe to him with confidence, further buildings in the region*".

Another building designed by Priestley—Porthall House, Lifford

of Ease and Palace, Derry; Strabane canal and new street layout for the Earl of Abercorn; Boom Hall, Co. Derry; and last but not least, a remodelling of the Bishop's Palace, Raphoe. Considering that *"in the mid-18th century there were very few native architects practising in Ireland as a whole, whilst fewer still in the more remote areas"*, Michael Priestley certainly left his mark in this part of the world.

The list of other structures attributed to this man is impressive. In 1774, the nephew of Thomas Connolly, M.P. and Speaker of the Irish House of Commons (1715-1729), is said to have commissioned Priestley to build Lifford House, which became the base for the Grand Jury during the Lifford Assizes. We know it today as the Gateway Hotel. Other famous buildings connected to him include Dunmore House, Carrigans; Prehen House, Co. Derry; Port Hall House, Lifford; Strabane Town Hall; Church of St. John, Clondehorky; Bishop Barnard's Chapel

Window detail

The Judge arriving at Lifford Courthouse c1910.

THE COURT IS IN SESSION

The following extract is based on an article by Seamus Ua Domhnaill which appeared in the Strabane Carnival booklet (1960). It gives us a flavour of what it was like when the court was in session at the end of the 19th century.

"For a day or two before the opening of the Assizes all available accommodation in Lifford was taxed to bursting point as Court officials, barristers, solicitors, jurymen, police and litigants sought lodgings for the three or four days over which the sittings usually lasted. Two judges travelled the circuit, one handling criminal proceedings while the other dealt with actions of equity. The latter cases were heard in the smaller courtroom now occupied by the Library. The judges and their personal staff stayed at Drumboy House, then owned by Mr Alexander Weir.

At a quarter to eleven each morning a gleaming black coach, drawn by four fine-stepping horses, bore the bewigged judges in their ermine trimmed robes to the Courthouse. The High Sheriff rode with them, and mounted police in front and behind provided an escort.

Forty or fifty sturdy constables of the constabulary in their spiked helmets had been in rigid attention under the critical eyes of the County Inspector and a couple of District Inspectors. When the coach drew up at the entrance, a liveried footman jumped down from the dickey and opened the door. A fanfare was sounded as their lordships alighted and proceeded with solemn judicial dignity to their chamber. Police saw to it that the public remained at a respectful distance from the entrances until their lordships passed through, but they were then permitted to enter the gallery and the back of the court in such number as the limited seating accommodation allowed.

To decide what cases should go for trial the Grand Jury held their deliberations in a large room upstairs. The Petty Jury, consisting of `twelve good men and true', sat in two pews on the left of the judge's bench. They were not allowed to have communication with anyone throughout the hearing and, if they failed to reach a decision before a reasonable hour, they

The Judge's coach arrives with mounted police escort at side entrance to Lifford Courthouse c1910.
'The Rookery' in the background

were obliged to spend the night locked up under constant guard.

While the old gaol was in use, prisoners were brought from it via an underground passage to the cells beneath the Courthouse. A look at one of these cells will bring home the awful conditions under which unfortunate human beings were doomed to spend years of confinement. In later years the prisoners were brought from Derry gaol in a closed black coach known as the `Black Maria' from which they were transferred to the cells below to await the calling of their cases.

When each man's turn came he was taken up a narrow stairway and hustled into the dock, which was an iron-barred enclosure facing the judge's bench. The gate of the dock was locked and the key placed in the custody of a burly policeman who stood guard there. As an additional precaution the prisoner was handcuffed to one of the two warders between whom he sat throughout the hearing. Many a man had his last look at the blue sky and the green slopes of Knockavoe as he gazed from this dock through the high window behind the judge's chair.

It is a pity that the records of the trials and tragedies enacted within its walls have not survived. Voices that rang through its corridors in bygone days have long since been stilled – voices raised in vicious accusation, in perjured testimony, and in dramatic defence".

Artist's impression of Judge's coach

POMP AND CEREMONY

Royal Irish Constabularly parade outside Lifford Barracks c1910.

Local R.I.C. Party at the opening of the Winter Assizes, Lifford 1913

A CURIOUS OLD CUSTOM

There was once a curious old custom that involved the old bridge at Lifford and the Courthouses at both Lifford and Omagh. In the 19th century if a jury could not reach a unanimous verdict in a case, they were sent to the `verge' of the county to be dismissed. In the case of Tyrone and Donegal the shared `verge' was the middle of the old bridge at Lifford.

The account below is taken from an old, undated newspaper cutting found in the Co. Donegal Archives collection.

"The two recesses on either side of the `curtain' wall [of Lifford Bridge] mark the dividing line between Tyrone and Donegal called the `verge' of the counties. A curious old custom was connected with them. If a jury in Lifford or Omagh disagreed with a verdict, the presiding judge had it in his power to send them to the verge of the county to be discharged. To a Lifford jury it was no great hardship but to an Omagh one, and especially in springtime, it was certainly a severe punishment on men who, acting on their oaths, had agreed to differ. The judge who, now-a-days would send a jury to this quaint spot to be released, would deserve to be crowned with cap and bells".

During our research we actually came across a case where this bizarre ceremony took place. On August 11th, 1827, The Strabane Morning Post recorded the following incident when, lock, stock and barrel, the judge, the prisoner and the jury upped-sticks and went to the middle of Lifford Bridge:

"Patk. Donnelly, indicted for the murder of John Beavers, on the 1st February last, near Dungannon. In this trial, the Jury retired at twelve o'clock on Friday morning, remained in one night, and on Saturday was removed, together with the prisoner, to Lifford Bridge, the verge of the County. Upon the arrival of Justice Torrens the Jury were called over, and not having agreed, the Judge then discharged the Jury, and stated he was sorry that they had been put to such inconvenience, more particularly as the great majority was of one opinion – eleven for conviction and one for acquittal – the prisoner was then ordered to remain in custody to next Assizes".

Patrick Donnelly was re-tried the following year and found guilty. He was finally hanged in March 1828 in front of the new gaol at Omagh and his body given to the surgeons for dissection.

The old Lifford Bridge

ROOMS TO LET

In the mid 18th century with the opening of the new Courthouse and the establishment of the Spring and Summer Assizes, life in Lifford changed, especially when the travelling circuit judges arrived. For the best part of a week before and during the hearings, accommodation was at a premium with lawyers, witnesses, policemen and the merely curious all looking for somewhere to stay.

There were several places, of various sizes, where the visiting throngs could find a bed and a bite to eat. At the top of the pecking order, the judges stayed at some of the 'big houses' in the area such as Drumboy. For the likes of lawyers, policemen and witnesses there was a choice of hotels. One of the oldest was called 'The Rookery', named after the large colony of birds which nested in the trees near the building. Built in the early 18th century on the site of Lifford Castle, it is believed to have been connected to the adjacent Courthouse by means of an underground passage. It continued to be occupied until 1967 when it was finally demolished. While it was being pulled down an interesting insight into 18th century building practices was revealed when "it was discovered that the inside walls were all composed of turf, neatly whitewashed over". The building which occupies the present site is known locally as 'Bannigan's Store' and is currently used by the County Council as a storeroom.

The Rookery

'The Rookery' next to the Courthouse prior to its demolition

Another substantial hotel was added to the town by the mid 18th century. Known first as Lifford House, it is attributed to Michael Priestley, the architect responsible for Lifford Courthouse. It was this hotel which became the base for the Grand Jury while the court was in session. When the railway network linking Strabane to both Derry and Belfast was completed in the 1850's the Grand Jury really arrived in style before they booked in. After they alighted at Strabane they *"were taken by horse-carriage the half-mile further to Lifford, accompanied by a military band"*. In 1878 when the business changed hands, it became known as Argue's Hotel. From those days until the present, the building has appeared in many guises, including a tea-blending warehouse, the head office of a newspaper, a bank and finally, a pub. Its present name is `The Gateway'.

Argue's Hotel in the early 20th Century

For those not so well off, and who wished to enter town without the hullabaloo, less salubrious but equally accommodating premises were also available. One of these was known originally as Sharkey's Tenements where, if you were in luck, a bed and a decent meal could be obtained at reasonable rates. Writing in 1821, John Graham commented *"Mr John Sharkey keeps a small but much frequented house for the accommodation of those who resort to the Assizes, sessions and gaol of Lifford from all parts of the country. Such are the happy days in which we live that when a shoal of herrings visited our shores in the spring of 1821, Sharkey was able to give plentiful dinners to his guests at two and a half pence a head"*.

Apart from the opportunity to make a few shillings still others saw it as a chance to have a bit of fun. Sometimes, however, things could get too lively. In September 1766 for instance, Lifford Corporation felt it had to put the foot down as matters were getting out of hand:

"Whereas the erecting of booths or tents at the time of the Assizes held in Lifford hath been generally productive of riot and disorder by encouraging drunkenness and quarrel, we therefore …to prevent such inconvenience for the future and preserve peace and good order in this corporation do order that in time to come no booth or tent be permitted to be erected and in case such should be erected by surprise or otherwise, that the person permitting the same on his or her ground shall forfeit 3 shillings and 4 pence for every such tent."

THE COUNTY GAOL

"Have you ever stopped to think what a powerful weapon a key is?"
Margaret Buckley

It is amazing to think there was once a time when being sent to prison was not seen as a punishment. Yet this was the case until the mid 1770's. Until then prisons were regarded simply as places were people were held until their trial. After their trial they were either set free, executed or transported. The onset of the American Revolution changed all that when the major destination for those prisoners who had been sentenced to transportation was suddenly no longer available. To alleviate the logjam of convicts a huge building programme of prisons was started and imprisonment as a punishment became more commonplace. This change in penal philosophy was reflected in sentences handed down in courts such as the Old Bailey when before 1775 only 2.3% of those on trial were sentenced to prison. Between 1780-1784 this had risen to 34.6%.

Cell window Lifford County Gaol

There was also a radical change in the internal operations of prisons. In the 18th century, law and order was seen as a local issue and paid for by the local taxpayer. Therefore Lifford, like the other forty prisons in Ireland at that time, was the concern of the local Grand Jury who looked after the building as a structure but had no control over the internal operations of the gaol. In the days when prison warders did not receive a wage this fell to the `Keeper of the Gaol' who regarded the prison as a private enterprise where the prisoners paid for everything and were the main source of income. At that time, even though a prisoner had served his sentence, it was possible for a gaoler to keep the prisoner in custody until his bill was settled. In other words, *"the prisons of Ireland were run as exploitive hostels. Prisoners were delivered into the hands of their gaolers as assets to be stripped, while rules were far less evident in the interior of prison walls than was the display of the Table of Fees."*

In 1786, however, there was a watershed when one of the most important pieces of prison legislation was passed. Under the influence of John Howard, `the founding father of the

The Day Room, Lifford County Gaol

modern prison', The Prison Act of that year not only laid down a set of rules by which gaols were to be regulated it was also a clear indication of what prisons were like prior to this legislation. Now, for the first time, Grand Juries were compelled to supply bread, fuel and bedding for the prisoners; the sale of alcohol was prohibited; cells were to be kept clean and white-washed twice a year; male and female prisoners were to be separated, as were the sick and healthy; chaplains and doctors were appointed; to eliminate extortion, the practice of taking `garnish money' was outlawed. *"This was an enforced tax imposed on the new prisoner, guaranteeing his safety in return for whatever money he had attached to his person. It was a strip-or-pay situation. If the new prisoner could not meet this demand, then his clothes were stripped forcefully from the person, leaving those already in dire need and want in a state of naked indignity. In fear of the seasoned prison bully, most newcomers succumbed to the pressure. The money obtained by the act of `garnish' would, whenever possible, be used to purchase illegal whiskey, readily available to the depraved prisoners at fourpence a half-pint from loitering hawkers"*. To further eradicate the exploitation of prisoners, additional legislation in the 1780's resulted in gaolers becoming salaried officials for the first time with a wage of £25 per year.

One of todays 'model' turnkeys at The Old Courthouse

THE PRISON REFORM ACT OF 1786

The present day in Lifford County Gaol

AN ACT FOR AMENDING AND CARRYING MORE EFFECTUALLY INTO FORCE THE SEVERAL LAWS NOW IN BEING FOR REGULATING THE PUBLICK GAOLS AND PRISONS THROUGHOUT THIS KINGDOM

It is requisite for the order and good government of prisons, and for the more effectually reforming abuses therein, that certain fixed specifick regulations should be adopted in every prison throughout this kingdom, to serve as rules for the conduct of inspectors, surgeons, medical assistants, gaolers, and other persons concerned therein: be it therefore enacted by the authority aforesaid, That from and after the passing of this act, the following regulations shall be carried into force in every gaol, house of correction, bridewell, and other prisons throughout this kingdom, that is to say:

1st. That it shall not be lawful for any woman to be keeper of any gaol.

2d. That every gaoler shall reside in his prison, and that he shall not be under sheriff, or a bailiff, nor shall he hold any office or employment that may require his attendance in any other place.

3dly. That no tap shall be kept in the prison, nor shall the gaoler, nor any person under his authority or appointment, directly or indirectly, sell to the prisoners any malt or spirituous liquors, or any manner of provisions whatsoever.

4thly. That the clergyman appointed to deliver out the common or county allowance of bread to the prisoners, shall attend the prison for that purpose three days in each week; he shall also take care that it is properly distributed according to the wants of the prisoners, and that it is of a good quality and proper weight, and that it is not more than forty eight hours since the same has been baked, and that he shall not suffer the prisoners to commute the said allowance, by receiving the value thereof in money, or in any other manner whatsoever.

5thly. That every room in the prison shall be daily scraped and swept, and that it shall be washed once a week in summer, and once a month in winter, and that twice at least in every year the inside of each of the rooms and cells of the prison shall be white-washed, viz one month before the lent and summer assizes respectively, and that sufficient bed-steads, ticken for beds and blankets, be provided for such prisoners as are in want of covering; and also, that sufficient fuel shall be provided for the common hall or halls of every such prison respectively, and that every prisoner shall be supplied with fresh straw once in every month.

6thly. That the prisoners who are sick shall be separated from those who are in health, and the surgeon or medical assistant shall regularly attend the former and supply them with medicine, and also with broth, or other necessary sustenance.

7thly. That debtors shall be separated from felons and other offenders, and that persons charged with highway-robbery, housebreaking, murder, or other capital offences, shall not be suffered to have any intercourse with prisoners confined for offences which are not capital, and that men and women prisoners of every denomination shall be kept separate.

8thly. That in every gaol there shall be one or more sufficient, clean and well secured yards for the convenience of prisoners, also a bath and one or more necessary to which the prisoners shall have free access; that no hogs, horses, cows, or other cattle, or poultry of any kind, shall be kept in the said yard; and that all prisoners shall be admitted at proper times in succession to air themselves in such yard or yards, for at least two hours every day, except prisoners under sentence of death, and such persons as are riotous or disorderly, or where there may be sufficient reason to apprehend that an escape may be attempted.

9thly. That no prisoner, even when condemned to death, shall be put into a dungeon or room under ground, unless in consequence of outrageous conduct, or for an attempt to break gaol.

10thly. That no spirituous liquors of any kind, shall be admitted into the prison on any pretence whatsoever, unless by a written order from the physician, surgeon, apothecary, medical assistant, or inspector, or any penny-pot, or garnish be taken from prisoners on their entrance into prison, on any account or pretence whatsoever.

11thly. That a table of fees shall be made out by the inspector general of prisons, and the inspector of prisons in the county of the city of Dublin, to be laid by them before his Majesty's court of king's bench, which table, if it shall be approved by said court, shall serve as a general regulation for fees throughout this kingdom, and the inspector general of prisons shall distribute copies thereof to the several county inspectors, to be by them placed in a conspicuous part of the prisons under their inspection; and the inspector general of prisons shall likewise cause several copies of this act to be printed on one side of a sheet of paper, and pasted on boards, which he shall also distribute among the several county inspectors to be by them placed in the common hall of every prison.

12thly. That the several local inspectors of prisons shall each of them visit the gaol or gaols under his inspection twice at least in every week; that at each visit he shall go into every room in the prison, and if any complaints are made by the prisoners against the gaoler or his agents, the inspector shall immediately enquire into the particulars of such complaint and report accordingly.

13thly. That the said inspectors shall each of them report specially on oath in the manner herein directed, the state of the prisons under their inspection respectively, to the magistrates at the quarter sessions, and likewise to the judges at the lent and summer assizes, and they shall also, twenty-one days at least before the sitting of parliament, transmit a similar report, together with a calendar of the prisoners actually in custody, setting forth the particular crime for which each prisoner has been committed, and likewise a general statement of all prisoners who have been tried, whether acquitted or condemned, specifying the several crimes of which they were accused, and the sentences of those who may have been found guilty, to the inspector general of prisons, to be laid by him before both houses of parliament on the first day of each session.

These 13 rules were just the beginning. To regulate the prisons, more and more legislation was introduced so that by 1867 some prison rule books ran to 120 pages.

THE EXTREME SENTENCE OF THE LAW

THE CASE OF HALF-HANGED MacNAGHTEN

Artist's impression of MacNaghten

One of the earliest recorded public hangings associated with Lifford Courthouse is that of John MacNaghten in 1761. Such was the publicity surrounding the case that even though it is nearly 250 years ago, the incident is still remembered to the present day and is now part of the local folk-lore. It was in the newly-built County Gaol that MacNaghten was held while awaiting trial for the murder of his fifteen-year-old `wife' Mary Anne Knox. Apparently *"Lifford gaol had to be used to hold MacNaghten since the Strabane prison was not considered either secure enough or clean enough for such a prisoner"*.

Born into a wealthy family, the well-educated MacNaghten had gambled away his family fortune while still a young man and had even embezzled £800 to feed his addiction when he was Collector of Taxes in Coleraine. The M.P. for Donegal, Andrew Knox, took pity on him and invited him to stay at his house at Prehen, near Derry. While there, he was attracted to Knox's daughter, the young heiress Mary Anne and, unknown to her father, arranged a very dubious marriage ceremony.

Although the marriage was declared null and void, Knox decided to take the teenager to Dublin out of harm's way. Hearing of this MacNaghten planned to ambush the coach and abduct the young girl. In the skirmish that followed, however, he mistakenly shot and killed Mary Anne while she was trying to shield her father.

After a fierce struggle and an attempt to take his own life, MacNaghten was finally captured and brought to Lifford. On the 7th of December 1761, MacNaghten, suffering from gunshot wounds received in the fracas, was carried into the Courthouse to face trial. Found guilty, at 1pm on the 15th of December he was led from the jail to be hanged. At the first attempt, however, the rope snapped but despite encouragement from the assembled crowd to escape, MacNaghten climbed the ladder once more while making his famous remark that no-one would ever call him `half-hanged MacNaghten'. There was no mistake the second time and despite his final wish he is still known as `half-hanged MacNaghten' to this day.

Representation of an early type of gallows

READ ALL ABOUT IT

One of the earliest local newspaper accounts of a murder trial and a hanging at Lifford appeared in the Derry Journal of August, 1772. In a brief statement it reported *"on Thursday last at the assizes held at Lifford, came on the trial of the three Dougherties, the father, son, and son-in-law, charged with the murder of Mr. Armstrong at Carn in the county of Donegal, when the father was acquitted, but the other two were found guilty"*.

Two months later, an equally brief account appeared after the sentence was carried out: *"Tuesday last was executed at Lifford, Neal Dougherty, pursuant to his sentence for the murder of Mr. Armstrong some time ago at Carn in the county of Donegal. He appeared very penitent and resigned to his unhappy fate, and died a Roman Catholic in the 31st year of his age"*.

HIGHWAY ROBBERY

Two years later, newspapers began to give fuller accounts of criminal activity in the area. The following account describes a case of highway robbery in June 1774 at Barnesmore or, as it is affectionately known locally, `The Gap'.

"On Wednesday last, the first inst., as Mr. James Ferguson, shopkeeper in the town of Donegal, was coming to Ballybofey he was attacked at the Bridge of Barnesmore by two men and a woman. They first stabbed his horse, and then himself, with a knife, and dragged him some distance off the road, when they cut open his saddle-bags, and from thence took 68 guineas in gold, 10 English shillings, 24 ounces of broken silver, and 2 silver watches. Providentially the horrid transaction was discovered by a boy who was looking after some cattle on the mountain; otherwise Mr. Ferguson might have soon died of his wounds without any assistance, and the robbers escaped justice; but the same day, they with two of their accomplices, were taken at an alehouse not far from the spot where they

Barnesmore Gap in more peaceful times

committed the cold deed, and all committed to Lifford gaol. Mr. Ferguson's recovery is very doubtful, and the horse is dead".

The gang were tried at Lifford Courthouse on August 22nd and two of them were sentenced to be executed at the scene of the crime. This was not unusual. In fact, such sentences date back to our earliest recorded system of law. Some 6,000 years ago Law 21 of the ancient Sumerians stated that a housebreaker shall be put to death and buried at the point where he broke in. This is how the newspapers reported the trial:

"On Monday last, the 22nd inst., at the Assizes held at Lifford, for the County of Donegal, Patrick Gordon and Henry O'Neil were tried and found guilty of robbing Mr. James Ferguson, of the town of Donegal, and sentenced to be hanged on the 8th September next, at the bridge of Barnesmore, the place where the robbery was committed. At the same time, the wife of the said O'Neil was also tried for robbery, and found guilty; but she having pleaded pregnancy was examined by a jury of matrons, who gave their verdict that she was pregnant, whereupon her sentence was postponed until after her delivery. Two other men were tried for the same robbery, but acquitted".

Confirmation that the hangings were carried out at the scene can be found in the Grand Jury Presentments which also gives us an idea of the costs involved. There are two entries for 1774, the first is for £10 paid to the Sub-Sheriff, Peter MacDonagh *"for transmitting Patrick Gordon and Henry O'Neil to the Bridge of Barnesmore where they were hanged"*. The second entry was for *"£7 7s out of the savings of the County at large, to be paid to Thomas Young, Esq., to reimburse him the like sum expended in building the gallows at Barnesmore"*.

THE STEWART BROTHERS

"His Lordship then put on the black cap and pronounced the sentence of the Court. 'That you James Stewart and Alexander Stewart, be taken from the place where you now are to the place from whence you came – the jail; and on Saturday next, from that to the common place of execution, the gallows, and there hanged by the necks until you are both dead – that your bodies be then given to the Surgeons for dissection, and may the Lord have mercy on your souls'".

The "Common Place of Execution" — The front of Lifford Gaol

With these words, delivered on the 31st of March 1831, the fate of the two Stewart brothers for the murder of Martha and John Lytle was finally sealed. Even so, James was convinced he had not received justice and in a chilling climax to the trial he declared:
"If Almighty God, before whom I will soon be judged, ever permitted man to have revenge, I will have it after my death". Then pointing in turn to the judge and jury said, *"I will visit you, and you, and you, after my death"*.

To witness the execution, 12,000 people packed into Lifford Diamond and surrounding streets. The following extract, from a newspaper of the time, is a gruesome account of the hanging.
"At 4pm, the door of the fatal drop-room was opened, and the wretched culprits, dressed in white robes, appeared. Having been placed under the beam, they drew down their caps over their eyes and the drop fell. James died without a struggle – but the rope by which Alexander was suspended, broke: and he was precipitated to the pavement, a distance of 40 feet. He fell with the side of his head on his own coffin, which was broken: and he

rebounded off it a few feet. He was instantly carried in by two officers of the Gaol.

The executioner, also dressed in white, with the part that covered his face daubed over in black, soon put another and stronger rope over the block and again raised the drop.

In about 20 minutes from the time he fell, to the astonishment of the assembled multitude, Alexander again appeared, and walked out on the drop, more firmly than before. He took his place and the signal being given, the drop was again dropped, but it rested on the shoulder of James, who was pushed aside and Alexander was launched into eternity but not immediately.

The board slowly moved down, sliding along James's body. The knot of the rope had shifted round the chin of Alexander and he suffered dreadfully for several minutes. His whole body was convulsed; during the strangulation, he several times put his feet to the wall, and pushed himself from it with great force, his clothes burst open so that his naked breast was seen and the cap, not being altogether over his face, blood was seen flowing from the wound which he had received on the cheek, in the fall.

At length his hands fell, his body was seen to stretch and he hung motionless alongside his brother. After hanging for the usual time, they were cut down, and the bodies handed over for dissection".

EXHIBIT `A'

The hatchet

*I*n today's modern world of forensic science and DNA testing we tend to forget just how crude and primitive the process of criminal investigation used to be. A case in point arose in the trial of the Stewart Brothers, James and Alexander, held in Lifford in March 1831. Although it was never proved conclusively, the weapon supposed to have been used in the killing was a hatchet found at the Stewarts' house. On a closer examination of the case, as reported in the local press of the time, it is remarkable how such a crucial piece of evidence could be treated in such a slipshod manner. Most certainly it would not have been acceptable as a reliable piece of evidence if presented in a criminal prosecution today.

The story of `Exhibit A' begins on a wet and stormy night in the small hours of September 5th, 1830 when John Baird was woken by John Lytle's little boy who told him to get the police as the old man and his wife had been killed and the house set on fire. When the police arrived, Baird and an armed constable William Cluff, began scouring the countryside for the perpetrators.

About 5am they arrived at the Stewart household where their suspicions were aroused when they found James and Paddy Stewart sitting at the remains of a fire. They also discovered a wet coat, a pair of wet shoes and, alarmingly, that James was wearing a blood stained shirt and there was blood on his arm from elbow to wrist. Taking them prisoners, they tied them together with a handkerchief and, with the aid of a candle, continued to search the room where Baird found a hatchet leaning against the back wall. Baird *"thought by the light of the candle he saw something like blood upon it; it was rather dry"*. Bringing the hatchet with him, Baird, Cluff and the two Stewarts then set off in the rain to lodge the prisoners in the small gaol in Donegal Town.

On the road, Baird began to have doubts about the hatchet because *"if there was blood on it, the rain would have washed if off and after some time carrying it agreed with Cluff that it was not blood"*. The train of events which follow become even more bizarre. About half-a-mile from the Stewart house they met Sally Hazlett and for some reason, possibly for safe-keeping or to return it to the Stewart household or simply because he got fed up carrying it, Baird gave the hatchet to her. In her evidence Sally Hazlett stated that she *"received the hatchet from John Baird the morning the business happened; had it from Monday till Saturday; the neighbours examined it in her presence and found some white or grey hairs upon it"*. When cross-examined she added *"It was about Wednesday the hatchet was examined; saw nothing but hairs on it; a man named Virtue took it to the door for three or four minutes and returned it; will not swear whether it was before or after this they found the hairs on it; the hatchet lay under her children's bed; it might have got hairs on it there"*.

After six days, the police decided to reclaim the hatchet and sent P.C. Edward Chism to collect it from Sally Hazlett where he *"found two grey or light brown hairs upon it"*. It may seem unbelievable today but the hatchet and the "two grey or light brown hairs" were actually produced in court and used to condemn the two brothers who were found guilty and eventually hanged in Lifford Diamond in April 1831.

The hatchet also came to an ignominious end. According to one story, it was kept in the execution room of Lifford jail for many years before being finally thrown in the river.

ANOTHER HANGING AT LIFFORD

The terrible fate suffered by the Stewart brothers, especially Alexander, did not end with their execution. Along with his two brothers, Patrick Stewart was also accused of the murder of John and Martha Lytle on 5th September 1830. He was held at Lifford Gaol for 11 months before he was brought to trial, where he protested his innocence to the bitter end. On being asked by the Clerk of the Crown what he had to say that sentence of death and execution should not be passed on him, the prisoner replied that he was *"as innocent of the crime as the child unborn"*.

His words had no effect, however, and four months after the execution of his brothers another Stewart stepped forward to face a hangman who had the added responsibility of operating a 'new drop' or scaffold which had been specially erected for the hanging. *"The spectators on the occasion were not so numerous as was expected, owing probably to such a scene having lost its novelty by the execution of his two brothers at the previous*

Assizes. The unfortunate culprit came forward to the platform with an unusually firm step, and without any apparent embarrassment, and in a voice neither weak nor tremulous, declared that he was totally innocent of the crime for which he was about to suffer. He said he forgave those who had been the means of bringing him to such a situation, and requested the multitude to pray for him.

We feel horror in relating, that, on his being launched, the rope, as in the case of his brother Alexander, gave way, and the unfortunate man was precipitated to the pavement – a distance of about thirty feet! – He was in a few moments taken up, and again put forward on the platform, without having sustained by the fall any perceptible injury; and on his being launched the second time, the divisions of the grating through which he descended, opened so slowly (in consequence perhaps of the stiffness of their hinges), that he literally slid into eternity and underwent STRANGULATION rather than HANGING, as the word is usually understood".

With regard to the erection of a `new drop' at Lifford it is stated that in the record room of the prison there used to be a model of a scaffold which a hangman named Murphy sent over from Glasgow to guide the Lifford carpenters in creating their terrible engine of death. Apparently, the model was an extremely neat one, and the delicate iron lever, which drew the bolt and caused the trap to open, worked perfectly. From reading the report in the paper about the execution, we can gather that the real thing didn't work perfectly and there was nothing delicate or neat about Patrick Stewart's death on Lifford's `new drop'.

SAMUEL AND PEGGY CRUMMER

During the Famine month of March 1847, The Derry Journal reported the trial of Samuel and Peggy Crummer who were charged with the wilful murder of Samuel Crummer, the elder, at Summy, Ardara.

Father and son had lived happily together until Samuel junior married Peggy in May 1845 against the wishes of his father, she being a servant of the family and of a different religion. Peggy was Samuel Crummer's 2nd wife. His first was the sister-in-law of Andrew Davis who later testified against them in court. From his address to the crowd before he was hanged, we gather he may have had children with her, but what happened to them we can find no mention.

There was a lot of ill feeling amongst the parties, the father was an old infirm man and suffered a lot of abuse from his son and daughter-in-law from the time of their marriage until his death in February 1846. Early in 1846, Samuel senior had made an arrangement with a neighbour, Samuel Cromer, to buy the farm for £100. This action enraged the son who said, *"he would take a life or lose his own,"* before he would be put out of the farm.

On Saturday evening the 14th February 1846, the old man was seen going into his house in the usual health and was never seen alive again. On the Sunday evening the old man was missing and neighbours, knowing the bad feeling between father and son and the unsatisfactory answers to questions as to where the old man was, had a strong suspicion of Samuel junior and Peggy having done something to him. On searching a lake near the house on the Monday morning they found the body of the old man at the bottom of a deep pool, with a chain fastened around it and attached to a large stone of considerable weight. After examination it was obvious that he had died a violent death.

Samuel Brown who was called to the stand recollects that he was passing by the old man's house at about two or three o' clock and saw him in his usual health. The next time he saw him was lying on the bed in his house, bound with an iron chain, dead!

A month before, Samuel Brown visited Samuel

senior and found him crying; the old man showed him black lumps on his hands and said his daughter-in-law had struck him with a stick. She retorted that, *"if I struck him he must have deserved it"*. Samuel junior was sitting on the bed-side and said nothing when his father told Samuel Brown that his son had pushed him to the back of the door in his room, took him by the private parts and tried to kill him. Several witnesses in court at the time also testified to seeing or hearing the old man being mistreated by his son and his wife.

On the Monday morning the sergeant of police went with others including the magistrate Mr. Hamilton, to the lake which was a little distance from the house where they observed an upturned stone, some straw with blood on it and in the direction of the house they observed the footprints of two persons, large ones as those of a man and smaller, barefoot ones, as those of a woman.

After being taken from the lake and removed to the house, the body was examined by the surgeon, Christopher Mc Garvey. He found a contused wound on the back of the skull sufficient to cause death, two incised wounds inflicted with a sharp knife or dagger on the left eye and on the side of the face. The lower jaw was fractured; there was a compound fracture of the arm, and chest and a left rib were broken.

In defence of the prisoners James Doherty Esq. addressed the jury and reminded them that the only evidence was circumstantial, *"no eye saw the deed committed, save the all seeing eye of heaven!"*

Baron Penefather also talked to the jury and told them they didn't need to go over the notes in case the reading would remove the impression which had been left on their minds by hearing and seeing for themselves, there was no doubt that the old man had suffered a violent death and it was up to them to decide at what time and by whom the deed had been done.

The jury retired and in less than an hour returned a verdict of guilty. The trial lasted from 12 o' clock until past eight o' clock on the evening, and excited the deepest interest. The Courthouse was crowded in every part, and the people had difficulty suppressing their emotions of horror as the details of the murder unfolded, especially when the chain and stone that had been attached to the old man's body were produced.

On Monday 15th March 1847, Samuel and Peggy Crummer were brought to the bar before Justice Penefather. *"Samuel exhibited a stolidity which, under the circumstances, can only be ascribed to that state of intellect which is little above idiocy, and may be designated brutishness. His wife was in tears. The prisoners expressed a fear that they may be transported! When the clerk put the question as why they should not be put to death, the wife looked piteously to her husband and said something to him; on which he replied, `I do not know a word that the man is saying.' The judge having assumed the awful emblem of death, (the black cap) then addressed the prisoners, telling them that, after a full and patient investigation, a jury had found them guilty of the foul crime of murder – a murder committed in anger and revenge. The judge advised them to take the remainder of their time to make peace with God. He was sorry to say that he could see nothing in their case to justify the smallest hope that mercy could be extended to them in this world. His lordship concluded by sentencing the prisoners to be severally hanged by the neck until dead, and their bodies to be buried within the precincts of the prison. His lordship afterwards fixed the first day of April as the day of execution. Samuel Crummer said nothing during his lordship's address only to raise his eyebrows in a look of surprise when he heard the words `hanged by the neck'. Peggy Crummer seemed to hold well together during the address but, on being removed from the dock, her cries could be heard from below, which were those of the bitterest agony; and we understand that she had to be conveyed to the prison in an almost insensible state".*

Samuel Crummer was hanged on April 30th, 30 days later than the judge had requested. His wife's punishment was commuted to transportation for life. Where she was transported to is not recorded, possibly Van Diemen's Land, but she would have been held in prison for at least a year as transportation was suspended between 1846-1848.

THE LAST PUBLIC EXECUTION IN LIFFORD

The following account is an extract from The Derry Journal May 1847:

"The extreme sentence of the law was carried into effect on Friday at Lifford on Samuel Crummer, who had been found guilty at the late Assizes for the county of Donegal, of the murder of his father, near Ardara, in that county. His wife had also been convicted together with him of the same offence, but the prerogative of mercy was exercised in her favour by the Lord Lieutenant, and her punishment was commuted to transportation for life. The evidence against both was circumstantial, but it was so conclusive that a most intelligent jury returned the verdict without hesitation, and the wretched parricide made no protestation of innocence upon his conviction. Since then his demeanour has been that of a stolid, illiterate man, who appeared to be quite insensible to the awful situation in which he was placed; but he has recently been heard to declare that his wife could prove that he was innocent, and that some members of her family were the perpetrators of the horrible and barbarous murder for which he was doomed to suffer. The wretched man was asked on Thursday whether he wished to see his wife, but he replied that he did not, remarking that she had been a bad wife for him. No sympathy was manifested for him, so fully persuaded were his neighbours and the public at large that he had committed the crime; and the circumstance of his intended execution excited so slight a sensation, although 14 or 15 years have elapsed since a similar event took place in the county of Donegal, that no more than three or four hundred persons were assembled at 11 o'clock at which time it was expected to occur, and the entire concourse present at 12 o'clock did not exceed a thousand persons, a large proportion of them being boys, and (we are happy to say, for the honour of the sex) very few females.

At twenty minutes before twelve, a strong party of constabulary, and sixty men of the 38th depot, were marched to the open space in front of Lifford Gaol, forming a semicircle, to prevent the crowd from approaching the building, and the fatal rope was seen attached to the metal bar above the drop. As the sub-Sheriff had *been instructed not to admit strangers to the prison, we cannot describe the particulars of what happened within its precincts, but we learned subsequently that Crummer partook of breakfast, with an apparent appetite, at eleven o' clock and that he exhibited no trepidation as the time drew nigh for his execution. While the hangman was putting a large white garment over his ordinary dress and pinioning his arms, he repeated aloud "Lord have mercy on my soul," and before he was conducted to the scaffold he shook hands with the Sheriff and the officers of the prison, to whom he returned thanks for their conduct towards him during his incarceration.*

At 12 o'clock precisely he was led out on the drop in front of the gaol, stepping with a cautious but firm tread on the iron grating. A thrill of horror ran through the multitude, and a murmur not of pity but of awe, was heard as he appeared. It was a spectacle that might well appal the stoutest heart, to behold a man of colossal proportions, in full health and vigour, and who had scarcely yet arrived at the meridian of life, and to know that in another minute or two he would be launched into eternity. He was six feet two in height, and but thirty-two years of age, although an imprisonment of more than twelve months, and the ghostly habiliments he wore, made him look several years older. But if anything could heighten the awfulness of the scene, it was the statement he made on the occasion. The executioner having adjusted the rope, the culprit proceeded to address the crowd in a loud voice, and in a firm and collected manner – `Gentlemen and ladies,' said the wretched man, `I am going to inform you that I am about to die, and I wish to tell you that I am innocent, and that I never lifted hand or foot to my poor father, nor would I do it, but ——, of Ardara, swore my life away for a little money in these hard times. I leave my blessing to my children and all my friends, and I forgive all as I hope to get forgiveness myself'. We were unable to catch the name of the individual to whom he alluded as having sworn away his life, owing to the screams of a female of weak intellect in a distant part of the crowd, who cried and gesticulated violently while the prisoner was speaking. The executioner, who was brought from Dublin for the purpose, then drew the *white cap over his face, when he remonstrated, and, turning towards the door, through which he had walked to the drop, he asked to see the governor of the gaol. The Roman Catholic priests who attended to prepare him for death, the Rev. Mr. Browne, of Strabane, and his coadjutor, the Rev. Mr M'Geoghegan, were standing at the door, and the latter addressed some words to him in Irish, and when Mr. Fenton, the governor, told him that it was usual to have the face covered, the priests desired him to be resigned, and one of them patted him repeatedly on the shoulder. Crummer then stood erect on the platform, with his front towards the street, and after a few seconds, which seemed to be passed in prayer, the bolt was drawn, and almost instantaneously life appeared to have left him. There was one convulsive movement of his arms after he fell, but it was only for a moment, and then he hung motionless. One of the policemen on duty was so much affected at the dreadful sight that he was led away in an almost fainting state. After the body had been suspended for three quarters of an hour, it was lowered and deposited in a coffin by the hangman, and immediately afterwards it was interred within the precincts of the prison".*

Site of the last public execution in Lifford. The front of Lifford Gaol prior to its demolition In 1907

BOUND FOR BOTANY BAY— 200 YEARS OF TRANSPORTATION

Botany Bay and **Van Diemen's Land** – whether or not your knowledge of geography is good, these are places that Irish people, even today, instantly recognise and associate with banishment and exile, pain and sadness. In song after song the names constantly crop up. Lines like the hugely popular:

She'll live and hope and pray,
For her love in Botany Bay,
But it's so lonely round the fields of Athenry.

However, Botany Bay and Van Diemen's Land only represent the last 60 years of the transportation system. The idea was first introduced 140 years earlier by Henry, the 4th son of Oliver Cromwell when, in the 1640's and 1650's, thousands of Irish people were shipped to the strange and distant shores of the West Indies *"on a royal order of banishment, issued lavishly as a merciful alternative to hanging"*.
This dense human traffic continued throughout the 18th century although, by then, the destination had changed – this time to America. From the regulatory Transportation Act of 1718 until 1775 it is estimated that some 13,000 Irish convicts were sent across the Atlantic, mainly to the labour intensive plantation colonies of Maryland and Virginia.

The American Revolution of 1775-1783 changed all that when all connections with the mother country were severed. This caused a problem on this side of the Atlantic. With nowhere to be transported, it resulted, for the first time, in large numbers of criminals being sentenced to the *punishment* of imprisonment. In turn this led to a rash of jail construction to accommodate the prisoners that lasted well into the 19th century. Before that, prisons were regarded as places of detention for debtors or holding centres for those awaiting trial, after which prisoners were either acquitted, transported or hanged. Towards the end of the 18th century imprisonment as a sentence gradually became the norm.

However, the age of transportation was not over and was re-introduced in 1787. The destination this time was firstly Australia and then Tasmania, with the first Irish shipload of 130 men and 22 women setting sail from Queenstown in April 1791.

Over the next 60 years until 1853, when transportation to Van Diemen's Land finally ceased, 200 ships were engaged in the business of transporting 30,000 men and 9,000 women from Ireland. Other figures suggest that the scale was even higher. In his study of hanging, V. Gatrell estimates that between 1787 and 1839, 113,200 people were sentenced to transportation at the English and Welsh assizes. Of this total, one-third were Irish.

A further increase in the numbers of those shipped overseas comes from an unusual source considering that transportation was *"as dreadfully feared as the death sentence"*. These additional figures represent the wives of transported felons who petitioned the authorities to be transported with their husbands. The pleas were often granted for two reasons. Firstly, it was seen of long-term financial benefit because it saved on the poor rates and secondly, by the 1830's there was a shortage of females in the transportation colonies. Despite the numbers involved, in reality many of these unfortunate `convict wives' and their husbands never reached their destination. With conditions on board the ships little better than those of slave ships, one fifth of this human cargo died at sea.

As in all aspects of Irish life, the Great Famine of the following decade also had an impact on transportation with a huge surge in the numbers `banished beyond the seas'. In 1845 there were 625 prisoners transported from Ireland. As the famine spread and intensified, tens of thousands committed crimes to get into prison to obtain food and shelter. Even a 20% reduction in the prison diet proved ineffectual as a deterrent. By 1849, 100,000 people were crammed into Irish prisons and transportation had increased five-fold to over 3,000. In some cases, prisoners even asked to be sent overseas in a desperate attempt to escape the tragedy unfolding in Ireland.

LIFFORD AND THE PENAL COLONIES

Apart from the death sentence, transportation was the most severe punishment handed out in the Courts of Ireland. Over the years, vast numbers of Irish men, women and children were shipped 'beyond the seas' to various penal colonies throughout the British Empire. The Cromwellian suppression of the 1641 rebellion alone, for instance, saw 12,000 people transported to the West Indies. In the 1650's thousands more, displaced and made destitute by upheaval, were shipped to the same destination.

Between 1718-1775, another 13,000 Irish convicts were sent to the American Colonies with at least two-thirds ending up in the plantations of Maryland and Virginia. In the final wave of transportation, from 1791-1868, a further 39,000 were delivered to Australia and Van Diemen's Land, later renamed Tasmania. Lifford, like all Assize towns, played its part in this cheap 'solution' to criminal activity in Ireland. The earliest record we have uncovered so far is based on the *Report of the Irish House of Commons into Enforced Emigration to America'*. This lists the 'convict felons and vagabonds' transported from the four separate Provinces over an eight-year period from 1735 to 1743. It also gives details on how much it cost each county to send them across the Atlantic.

Leinster, and especially Dublin, provided the greatest number of felons and vagabonds. At a cost of three thousand eight hundred and seventy pounds, nineteen shillings and tuppence (!), 937 people were transported in 8 years. This was more than the other three Provinces put together. Next came Munster with 542. Then Ulster – 296 – and finally Connaught with 145 transported.

In the Ulster league table, Donegal came joint third with Co. Down, having 42 transportees – 38 men and 4 women – costing £240 for the period. Interestingly, compared to the 19th century, only two types of crime are listed, either 'Grand Larceny' or 'Vagabond'.

From other local records such as the 18th century Grand Jury Presentments, we are able to break down the costs of transportation even further. One entry for 1754, for example, reads:

£1 10s 0d to Archd. McCrea, Lifford gaoler, for taking John Winsley to Derry. 10/- to Ralph Brook, Derry gaoler, for bringing John Winsley back to Lifford. £10 to be levied and paid to Chris Carleton Esq. for transporting John Winsley.

Other entries for 1757 and 1758 include:

£1 to Isaac Armstrong, gaoler, for transmitting John McCaristin and Jeritt Laird from Lifford Gaol to Derry to be transported. £10 to Henry Sloan, under sheriff of Donegal for transporting John McCaristin and Jeritt Laird to some of his Majesties Plantations in America.

£7 0s 10d to Henry Sloan, late under sheriff, to reimburse him for submitting Cornelius Strean, Thomas McConnel and Jeritt Laird and while in Derry Gaol under the rule of transportation for the hire of boats and a guard to put the said persons on board the various vessels.

By the turn of the century Australia and Van Diemen's Land were the latest, and last, destinations for transportees. Offenders found guilty of horse, cattle and sheep stealing were destined for these places. These were actually capital offences and punishable by death. However, this was eventually commuted to transportation for life.

Theft of any description and variously referred to as larceny, felony, stealing, burglary and robbery was the most common offence for which the sentence of transportation was handed out. In a survey of the Irish Transportation Registers for 1839 and 1840 it accounted for almost 75% of convictions. In that respect, Donegal was no different to any other part of the country where theft was also top of the list.

The severity of some sentences, however, did not seem to match the gravity of the crime. In 1831, for instance, Sarah McCoy was found guilty of stealing £50 and 180 shillings and transported for 7 years. The previous year, Bernard Kelly was convicted of stealing 3 shillings in Letterkenny and he received the same punishment. When he heard his fate Kelly called out to the judge, *"Please your Lordship, I hope you won't send me over alone"*. He wasn't disappointed because six others joined him – four of them for `Life'.

Other, seemingly trivial, offences which attracted a 7-year sentence include those listed on the facing page.

Anne Moore, for stealing clothes to the value of 10/-.
John Doherty, for stealing an 8st. sack of oats.
Lucinda Sweeny, for vagrancy.
Margaret McShee, for stealing two stuff dresses and one calico dress.
Sally McLaughlin, for stealing bedclothes.
John Gillespie, for receiving two yards of blue cloth, knowing the same to be stolen.
Rebecca Roarty, for stealing two caps.
Mary Cannon, for stealing 12 yards of printed calico.
Mary Hart, for having stolen a straw bonnet, shawl, and apron.
Eleanor Clendenning, for stealing a grey cloak.
Michael McFadden and Alexander McFadden, his son, for stealing 16 geese.
Thomas Mathews, for stealing a tobacco box, of the value of 1d, and tobacco, value 4d.
Jane Duddy, for stealing 5 chickens and 2 hens.
Francis McDaid, for stealing a handkerchief and blankets.
Catherine Barton, for stealing a piece of woollen cloth.
James Cassidy, for stealing plough irons.
John O'Donnell, for stealing a piece of cloth from a bleaching green.

O'Donnell seems to have made quite an impact at his trial. According to the local press:-
"The prisoner, in a cross examination of one of the witnesses, displayed a singular degree of talent and acuteness. His Lordship in passing sentence, observed, that it was a pity a person possessed of so much talent, had the misfortune to be charged with theft, and not have the power to apply such talent to a better purpose. Therefore, to prevent him from exercising such a talent in future in a similar way, he would transport him for seven years. The prisoner on leaving the Bar turned round and exclaimed, `Devil may care, it's nothing but a cobbler's apprenticeship anyway'".

If the gravity of the offence did not influence the sentence neither did the age of the offender. The following case was tried at Lifford Summer Assizes, 1828:-

*`Hugh Gallagher, 11 years old, for sheep stealing. The prisoner pleaded guilty.
The prisoner on being asked by the Court, if he knew the consequence of pleading guilty to a charge of sheep stealing, or if he knew that the punishment of the crime was transportation,*

replied in the negative. He then pleaded Not Guilty.

It appeared in evidence, that the prisoner had been connected with some persons in the neighbourhood, where he had stolen the sheep, and that he had offered them for sale for the sum of twelve shillings – Guilty – To be Transported seven years'.

This was not an isolated case. Stephen McGloughlin, *"a boy of about 12 years of age"*, was transported for 15 years for setting fire to an out-house. In his defence his older brother, Philip, claimed it couldn't have been Stephen because he was *"a great coward, and was afraid to go out at night lest the bogles (fairies) should take him"*.

Another boy of about 12 years of age, James Diver, was transported for seven years for stealing two promissory notes to the value of £8 5shillings. Mary Kelly, *"a very young girl from Ballyshannon"*, received the same sentence for having a stolen silver spoon in her possession. Her namesake, the *"very young"* James Kelly, was transported for the theft of one purse, one penknife, and coins to the value of £1 1s 11d and the 15 year old, Hugh Bradley, was sent `beyond the seas' for seven years for stealing a knife.

For most of these youngsters and their families the idea of being transported must have been terrifying. Yet, there was the odd case when some young offenders remained undaunted by the prospect. One example of this happened in 1839 when Anne McIntyre and Emily Richardson, *"both young girls"*, were transported for seven years for stealing clothes. On hearing the verdict they *"made a low curtsey, and thanked his Lordship, saying, `he could not do them a greater service, as they hoped to get a Black there.' They then retired in roars of laughter"*. This, however, was an exception.

OTHER FORMS OF PUNISHMENT

Apart from the extremes of execution and transportation the Court also handed out additional punishments to a prison sentence. The most common of these was hard labour, usually for the entire duration of the sentence. Like many other prisons throughout Ireland the usual form of hard labour was breaking stones which would then have been used to build and repair roads.

Another form of hard labour was pounding bones for manure. This fertilizer was then advertised in the local press and sold at the gaol as in the following which appeared in the *Strabane Morning Post* on May 4th, 1835:

> 300 Bushels of BONE MANURE to be Sold at Lifford Gaol, at 2s 3d per Bushel, for any quantity not less than 20 Bushels; under 20 – 2s 6d per Bushel. As the Turnip season is now come, an early application is recommended.
>
> N.B. The Bone is reduced to dust.

A more public, painful and humiliating punishment was whipping. Reminiscent of the hangings at the scene of the crime in `The Gap' during the 1770's, this was sometimes carried out in the town where the offence was committed. In 1823, for instance, John, Daniel, Michael and Owen McGarrigle, James McEntire and Charles Judge were sentenced to be imprisoned for one year for *"pulling down a house near Ballyshannon, the property of Mary McGarrigle"*. They were also *"to be publicly whipped through the town of Ballyshannon, from the bridge to the Fair Green on the 12th of April, 21st of June, and 18th of September"*.

During the Famine years when the theft of food was common, whipping was sometimes added as an additional deterrent, particularly if the offender was a young male like fourteen-year-old Edward Diven. For the theft of two sheep in February 1849 he was sentenced to nine month's imprisonment with hard labour. He was also to be whipped three times - on the first Monday of April, May and June. Later that same year, another fourteen year old, John

Kerr, was convicted of stealing a goose and sentenced to three months with hard labour and to be *"thrice whipped with a birch rod"*. As if in anticipation of the flogging, when he heard the judge's decision, *"the prisoner's countenance underwent the most extraordinary contortions on hearing the latter part of the sentence"*.

The Stone Breakers Yard, Kilmainham Gaol C1890. A similar scene would have been found at Lifford

THE MEN OF `98

GENERAL JAMES NAPPER TANDY

I met with Napper Tandy and he took me by the hand,
How is dear old Ireland, and how does she stand?
It's the most disgraceful country that I have ever seen,
They're hanging men and women for the wearing of the green.

Napper Tandy was one of Lifford's better known prisoners. A founder member of the United Irishmen he landed at Rutland Island off the Donegal coast in September 1798 on board the *Anacreon* with a consignment of arms and French troops. Discovering that the rebellion had already failed, he set sail back to the continent where he was arrested in Hamburg and eventually extradited back to Ireland, first of all to Kilmainham in Dublin, and then finally to Lifford. At his trial he pleaded guilty to the charge of treason and was sentenced to be hanged, drawn and quartered. Fortunately for the General, Napoleon Bonaparte interceded on his behalf and refused to sign a peace treaty which had been agreed between France and Britain unless Napper Tandy was released. His sentence was eventually commuted to transportation for life and then further reduced to exile. He was finally released into the care of his son and arrived at Bordeaux in March 1802 where he died the following year, aged 63, and was buried with full military honours.

James Napper Tandy, relaxing with one of his visitors over a glass of wine in his `miserable dungeon', Lifford 1801

CAPTAIN MANUS O'DONNELL

Life in prison at the end of the 18th century could be harsh, depending on the wealth and connections of the prisoner. Napper Tandy, for instance, was accused of living boisterously while at Lifford. He was excused from work and allowed to receive visitors, including his wife who stayed with him for a time during his confinement. For others, like Manus O'Donnell it was a different matter. Born in Kilmacrennan in 1758, Manus had joined the United Irishmen and by 1798 had been elected to the position of Captain. Acting on information supplied by a local informer, however, he was arrested and taken prisoner to Letterkenny where he was *"fettered, neck and foot"* and placed in solitary confinement for a month. To extract information *"He was only allowed one pint of water and a crust of bread each day. Thumbscrews were put on him which, besides causing much pain, resulted in the loss of great quantities of blood. A coffin was placed in his cell and famished rats that ate the thongs out of his boots were put in to keep him company ...but it was all in vain, Manus remained silent"*.

Without further interrogation, he was then transferred to the `New Gaol' at Lifford but *"the change brought little improvement in conditions. The food was bad and barely sufficient to keep body and soul together. The prisoners were permitted a quarter of an hour's exercise in the yard each day and their hunger used to be so great that they pulled and greedily devoured any weeds or blades of grass they could find growing at the base of the wall"*.

Unlike Napper Tandy's trial, Captain O'Donnell was brought before a military tribunal which used to sit in the Grand Jury room on the second floor of the Courthouse. The case against Manus collapsed, however, when the informer and principal Crown witness failed to put in an appearance at the court. To resolve this embarrassing situation, Captain Murray, as head of the tribunal, found what he thought to be a satisfactory solution. He offered Manus his freedom if he would fight a mounted dragoon. To defend himself he was only allowed to use a pike, a commonly used weapon of the time.

As news of the impending duel at Lifford spread, *"the biggest crowd that was ever seen

Manus O'Donnell's birthplace near Kilmacrennan c1928

in the county is said to have assembled to see Manus match his skill with the dragoon on that memorable day in March, 1799". In the event, his supporters were not disappointed when Manus, with two deft manoeuvres, managed first to cut the reins of the dragoon's horse, and then to bring the horseman unceremoniously to the ground.

Instead of being released as promised, however, Captain Murray decided to further punish Manus and ordered him back to Lifford prison to receive 500 lashes. Fortunately, for Manus, Lord Cavan, in overall command of the forces in the area, happened to be passing through Lifford on his way to Letterkenny. When he heard what had happened he overturned Murray's orders and Manus O'Donnell was finally released and returned triumphant to Kilmacrennan where he lived to the ripe old age of 86 years old. The following ballad based on Manus's exploits appeared about 100 years after the event.

A FIGHT FOR LIBERTY

Let me tell of a deed of daring, done in gallant Ninety Eight,
By a son of bold Tir-Conaill, who had won the Saxon's hate.
For the base spies had betrayed him as a leader in the land,
High in council, high in courage, fit to follow or command.

So, before the green flag floated in rebellion on the gale,
Shackled Manus Mor O'Donnell captive lay in Lifford gaol.
And the rising did not prosper, and the British breath'd again,

Young Wolfe Tone is dead in prison, scattered the United Men.

Spake a Captain then to Manus, "Rebel, we will set you free
If you fight a British soldier, your pike science we would see."
So they picked a vet'ran, a dragoon in coat of mail,
With his trusty long-pike by him rebel Manus did not quail.

In the green holm, where the Modhaim joins the gently flowing Finn,
There between Strabane and Lifford, they are ready to begin.
Shouted, stentor-like, a clansman from the bridge below Strabane,
"Buaidh Ui Dhomhnaill, buail go cliste, gabh do phice, 'nois go teann."

Spurred the horseman then his warhorse, and he brought the lance to rest,
Levelled, while his war horse prances, at O'Donnell's naked breast.
But the Gael with ashen handle of his pike thrust in the ground,
As his foeman charges forward, leaps aside with airy bound.

Then like circling eagle wheeling, strikes the rider's bridle rein,
Deftly, lightly with his pike-axe cuts the leathern straps in twain.
And with back-blow fixes pike-hook in the rider's mail breast,
Drags him to the green sward, lightly plants his foot upon his chest.

Scorning then to spill his life blood, from him turns upon his heel,
And as token to his comrades waves aloft the flinting steel.
Faith of Saxon promise learns he, though he knew its value well,
He is dragged again to prison, locked within the narrow cell.

But the noble Earl Cavan hears the tale and comes to see,
And distaining faithless vengeance, nobly sets O'Donnell free.
Peacefully he lived his life out, and his grandsons now are men,
Who would follow in his footsteps, did the troubles come again!

LITTLE STORIES FROM THE COURTHOUSE

Throughout the 19th century, many important cases were heard in the Courthouse including the trial of Francis Bradley who spent two years in prison before he was finally cleared of the murder of Adam Grierson, agent for the evicting Glenveagh landlord John Adair. There was also the famous Lord Leitrim murder case which saw one of the main suspects, Michael Heraghty, fall victim to typhus in Lifford gaol before his trial came to court. Despite the lack of official court and prison documents these high profile cases have already been well documented and have appeared both in print and on film. Yet, over the years, there were thousands of cases heard in the Courthouse of which we know very little. This includes not only the Assizes, which at least warranted some mention in the newspapers of the time, but all of the Quarter Sessions which were not covered at all. Take, for example, one of Donegal's most common offences, illicit distillation or poteen-making. At the March Assizes of 1827 alone, no fewer than 210 men and women were sentenced to between three and six months imprisonment. Apparently, the crime was so prevalent and the prisoners so numerous that the newspapers did not even bother to list their names.

On occasion we are given other tantalizing glimpses of the social and economic conditions in 19th century Ireland such as the following brief account of, perhaps, Lifford's youngest prisoner. In July 1836, *"Charles Gorman, a chimney sweep, and John Breen, his apprentice, a child of about seven or eight years of age, were found guilty of stealing a body coat. They presented a most miserable appearance, being almost in a state of complete nudity; but between them a conflict of generosity occurred, which was creditable to their feelings. The young fellow insisted that he alone was guilty of the theft, his master having been wholly ignorant of it; while the master urged that it was he only who ought to suffer, as he had counselled the theft and the boy was not to be blamed for obeying his orders.*

The learned Judge, with a view to the improvement of the boy's morals, sentenced him to six month's imprisonment, he being permitted to attend the school. Gorman was sentenced to a week's imprisonment".

Despite the importance of newspapers as a primary resource, in most cases very little supplementary information is available for the countless number of men and women who appeared in the dock at Lifford Courthouse. At the very best, their names (sometimes misspelled), crime and sentence are all that remain of their brief interlude in the public eye. Even this basic information raises the odd question mark such as this terse statement from 1827, *"James Henry, for murder – to be imprisoned one week"*. Another example is that of horse-thief, Patrick Munday, whose total press coverage in 1823 amounted to simply, *"sentenced to be executed on 6th of May"*. A hanging usually guaranteed some press coverage but apparently not in Patrick Munday's case as his name does not appear in print again. All we can assume is that the sentence was commuted to transportation for life which was not unusual for this type of offence. In July 1834, a similar fate was also handed out to Margaret McCallion, described

The chimney sweep's apprentice

as *"about 35 years of age with a sallow visage which is deeply scarred with small pox"*. Before Chief Justice Doherty, she was found guilty of having set fire to a house. *"The prisoner being asked what she had to say why sentence of death should not be passed upon her, made no answer; and his Lordship proceeded to address her. He implored her to prepare for the great change from time to eternity, as he had no reason to entertain the smallest hope of mercy being extended to her on this side of the grave. In submitting the case to a higher authority there was not a single circumstance he could state to induce a mitigation of her sentence. He now assumed the black cap and pronounced the extreme sentence of the law. Before his Lordship left Lifford, he ordered her to be executed on the 6th of September"*. Yet, once again, that is the last to be heard of Margaret McCallion and, like Patrick Munday, she probably was sent `beyond the seas.'

The severity of these sentences was not uncommon. In 1820 there were at least 200 offences which attracted the death sentence. In reality, however, and because of a gradual change in attitude, by the 1830's the death sentence was eventually reserved for serious crimes such as murder. Even so, until an Act of Parliament was passed, judges still had to officially record the death sentence for such offences as cow, horse and sheep-stealing.

THE LIFFORD ASSIZES 1830

To give an idea of the typical crimes and sentences in Donegal in the early 19th century the following is a list from a contemporary newspaper of 1830.

Edward Marley, for stealing a calf, the property of Thomas Johnston – Not Guilty.

Patrick Gallagher, for stealing a mare at Carrickmagorran, the property of Andrew Long, on the 18th January last – Sentence of death recorded.

Bernard Kelly, for taking 3s from the person of Charles Doherty, in the town of Letterkenny, on the 23rd of October last – To be transported seven years.

Margaret Henderson, alias McColgan, for stealing divers articles of wearing apparel, from the shop of James Hayes of Raphoe, on 28th of August last – To be imprisoned 3 months.

Robert Philips and George McElwain, for stealing a silver watch, the property of Wm McCrea, on the 28th September last, from his house in Ballybofey – Acquitted.

James Stewart, for stealing a quantity of oats, the property of Robert Little – Not Guilty.

John Gallagher, sen, John Gallagher, jun. and James Helferty, charged with maliciously wounding a mare, the property of George Bustard – Not Guilty.

Thomas Moore, for stealing two sheep, the property of John Adair and James Boyle, at Ardara - Guilty.

Margaret Kerr, for stealing a purse containing one sovereign and two promissory notes, from Andrew McBeth, on the 23rd of February, in Lifford - To be imprisoned six months.

Eleanor Doherty, for stealing a bond from Neal

McMullen, on the 3rd of January last at Marshyglen – Not Guilty.

Charles Brown, Sarah McGarrigle, and Catherine O'Farrell, for stealing out of the Distillery of John Morton, at Lifford, seven gallons of whiskey and seven or eight shillings from the desk in silver, on the 13th September last – Charles Brown and Catherine O'Farrell to be imprisoned twelve months and kept to hard labour. Sarah McGarrigle – Not Guilty.

Hugh Roarty, for stealing 10lbs of iron, the property of the Mining Company of Ireland, on the 1st of October, at Kildrum – To be imprisoned 12 months and kept to hard labour.

Owen Duffy, for uttering two counterfeit shillings, and Catherine Duffy, for having in her possession 18 counterfeit shillings, knowing them to be such, at Mt Charles, on the 13th of October last – Owen Duffy to be imprisoned six months; Catherine Duffy – Not Guilty.

James Crawford, sen., James Colville, William Morrow, James Crawford, jun., James Watson, Robert McVittie, Samuel Crawford, John Dinsworth, William Thompson, and A. McKinley, for riotously assembling in the town of Ardara on 1ST January last, with a fife and drum, and dressed with Orange ribbons, sashes, &c. armed with swords, and continuing assembled during the space of two hours — To be imprisoned one fortnight and kept to hard labour except Samuel Crawford – fined 6d and discharged.

John Shiel, for the murder of John McCarter, by striking him with a stone, of which he died, also for aiding and assisting John Gallagher in the murder of said McCarter, on the 23rd of September, at Labadooe — Guilty of Manslaughter, to be imprisoned 12 months and kept to hard labour.

Edward Gallagher, for cow stealing – Not Guilty.

James McSwine, for assaulting James McGinley at Ballymore – Not Guilty.

Elizabeth Mae, for having in her possession a forged note at Letterkenny – Not Guilty.

Catherine McDite, for offering a counterfeit sovereign to Bridget McMonagle, at Moneyreagh – To be imprisoned six months, and give security for good conduct for six months more.

Patrick McGinley, for stealing lead from a dwelling house of the Marquis Cunningham, on the 20th of Jan. last at Rutland – Not Guilty.

Andrew Given, for a riot at Donegal, on the 13th of July last – To be imprisoned one fortnight and kept to hard labour.

John Rankin and Thomas Irvine, charged with the murder of Patrick Ward at Pettigo, on the 28th of January last – Not Guilty.

Dominick Donald, for uttering base coin, at Pettigo, on the 25th of April last – Not Guilty.

Catherine Boyle, for having stolen goods, the property of Samuel Kerr, of Raphoe, in her custody – Guilty.

John McPaul, charged with selling sheep which had been stolen from John Ferry and Patrick McGhee, on 4th and 6th of May – Guilty of stealing them. Sentence of death recorded.

Daniel Boggs, for stealing a horse, the property of Mathew McIlwaine, on 3rd January last – Sentence of death recorded.

Margaret Stephenson, for passing base silver, at Creslaugh fair, on 10th of June last – To be imprisoned six months and kept to hard labour.

Joseph McGolrick, for stealing a horse, the property of James Semple, on the 20th of June last – Sentence of death recorded.

Eliza Loftus, for stealing wearing apparel, &c. – To be transported for 7 years.

Although the newspapers are invaluable, they did not cover every case. There are, however, two other sources which provide us with another insight into law and order in the past. The first of these are the old ballads which were hawked around the fairs and markets. Here is one example based on the story of Charles O'Boyle, a pilot from Rutland Island. Pilots were local men with vast knowledge and experience of the tides, rocks and reefs around the coast of Ireland and would be called upon by the captain of a ship to guide them to safe anchorage, especially in bad weather.

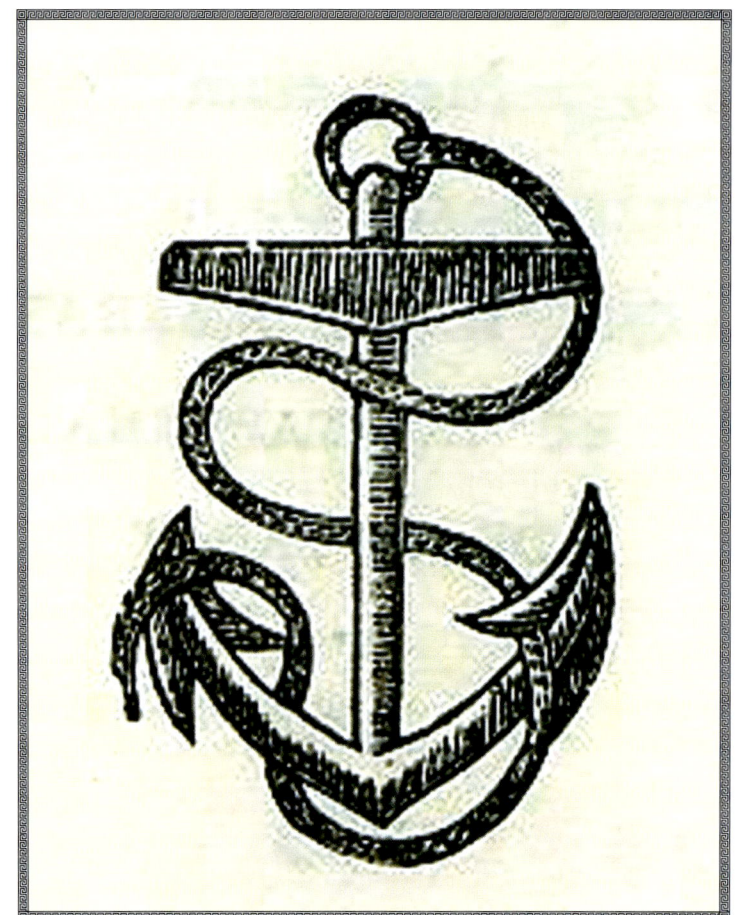

PILOT CHARLES O'BOYLE of RUTLAND ISLAND

One stormy night in winter, when the seas rolled mountains high,
A barque with all sails spread, O'Boyle the pilot, did espy.
"To the boat, my men", his order was "and hurried be ye all,
And try to save this distressed ship off the Coast of Donegal!"

The men complied with willingness; O'Boyle his skill did show,
By guiding his boat o'er shoals and reefs, while his men did ably row.
The barque she flew her signal – `Distress' it did proclaim,
And O'Boyle cried to his oarsmen "You are worthy of your fame."

The barque was reached in safety; O'Boyle on deck he sprung,
The captain warmly greeted him, saying, "Your work it is well done.
This barque I give you in command, to guide her safe to port,
You'll save our lives and cargo, if our ship you'll keep afloat."

O'Boyle he quick assented, to the captain he did say,
"Your barque will be in harbour safe by dawning of the day.
And for my risky labour and that of all my men,
You'll pay in golden guineas, a modest eight pounds ten."

The captain smiled vexatiously, and of a trap thought he,
Saying "O'Boyle, for breaking pilot rules, my prisoner you must be.
This rope in your possession, is from my barque *Mary Anne*,
Taken without permission, so your trial you must stand."

As prisoner to Lifford Court, the law did O'Boyle compel,
That brave and skilful pilot whom his neighbours loved so well.
The Judge he heard the accuser, and the jury to a man,
Agreed that the pilot was a very guilty one.

The sentence it was heavy, shocking people far and near,
Banishment from home and kin, and land he loved so dear,
To far off Van Diemen's Land, seven years he had to go,
The pride of Rutland Island, t'was a sad and cruel blow.

The Charles O'Boyle mentioned in the song would have come from a family with a long tradition of piloting in the North-West of Donegal, especially in the Arranmore and Rutland Island areas.

It was a Tadgh Boyle, for instance, that the captain of the *Anacreon* called for when landing Napper Tandy in 1798. As local historian, Belinda Mahaffy discovered, *"He had an expert knowledge of the entire west coast of Ireland and is reputed to have once taken a vessel as far south as Limerick, for which he was rewarded with a hat full of sovereigns, and walked the entire distance of more than 230 miles back home!*

Tradition says that once aboard the Anacreon a pistol was held to his head and he was informed that if he went off course, or failed to bring the craft to a proper place of mooring, his brains would be blown out. After Napper Tandy slipped off from Rutland Island in the Anacreon, pilot Boyle was duly arrested and arraigned at Lifford assizes. His defence, that he had been deceived by the ship flying the English colours, was successful and he was acquitted".

Not so fortunate was the pilot Charles Boyle who was arrested in 1825 and tried at Lifford Courthouse for `plundering a vessel wrecked off the island of Arranmore.' It was blowing a gale that November and his assistance had been requested by Captain John Taylor who was in command of the *Waller*, en route from Limerick to Liverpool with a cargo of wheat, flour, oats, tongues, whiskey and butter.

It was claimed in evidence that although the ship was being steered by the helmsman, Boyle gave directions which led them into the wrong channel where they drifted onto a rock and foundered. It appears that a musket was then fired as a signal to the islanders who swarmed on board and plundered the cargo.

Only one other person was charged with the offence but he was acquitted. Boyle, however, was found guilty and sentenced to be executed on the 4th of April, 1826. This was eventually commuted to transportation for life.

Another interesting source is folklore. The following account appeared in *Historical Sketches of Lifford* by John McCosker.

"This case took place in the black Famine year of 1847 when a man from the parish of Gartan was tried for killing a young man, a near neighbour and a distant relative of his own. They disputed about a right of way, and in a scuffle that took place between them the prisoner struck his opponent with a spade he had in his hand at the time, from the effects of which the young man died. The presiding judge was Doherty, the prisoner was Doherty, the man slain was Doherty, prisoner's solicitor was Doherty, and many of the witnesses were Doherty. He was found guilty of wilful murder and sentenced to be hanged within a month.

And now it was remembered that this prisoner was from the parish of Gartan, and that St Columbcille had prophesised that no person born in Gartan would ever be hanged. Would or would not the prisoner be hanged was the question in every person's mouth and excitement ran high when it came to within a day of the dread penalty of the law being carried out.

No reprieve had been received, and the finisher of the law was within the jail, and had all things in readiness for the performance of his ghastly work. But early next morning a courier arrived in Lifford, made his way to the jail, and delivered to the governor the Lord Lieutenant's warrant commuting the sentence to one of penal servitude for life. Whether St Columbcille made such a prophecy I do not know, but certain it is that no record or tradition exists telling of a single case of hanging of anyone belonging to the parish of Gartan".

Front elevation of the Courthouse

LEGENDS AND ESCAPES

DEAD OR ALIVE?

William Clements,
Third Earl Of Leitrim

In 1878, four men accused of the murder of 73-year-old William Sydney Clement, better known as Lord Leitrim, were lodged in Lifford jail. The overall story is already well known but briefly, three of the accused, the McGranaghan brothers, were kept in confinement for twelve months before being finally released due to lack of evidence. The exception was Michael Heraghty. The official story is that he died in the prison hospital on the 12th of October 1878 after suffering for 14 days with typhus fever.

This extract outlines some of the concerns of the jury during the inquest:

".every member of the jury raised strong objection to having to view the body as laid down by law. They pleaded that as deceased was a victim of a contagious disease, there was a risk of it being passed on to themselves or their families by any contact with the body. The Coroner, Mr John Weir, however, was adamant and sorely against their wills, the jury trooped in a body to the mortuary where the remains reposed. On their return, four of their number admitted they had not laid their eyes on the body and were promptly ordered by the Coroner to return and carry out their statutory obligation. This they did". His remains were released two days later and brought home for burial where the funeral became one of the largest ever seen in the Fanad peninsula.

All of this seems to be fairly conclusive, particularly after the formality of an inquest. Yet, despite the official version, there is another, more romantic story which claims that Heraghty had faked his death and that the coffin buried in Fanad was, in fact, empty. One oral account of the time states that his funeral was supposed to be *"the most cheerful cortege ever to leave Lifford"* and when the crowds dispersed at Drumboy they wished the `deceased' Godspeed because it was widely believed that Heraghty had escaped and was on his way to America where he eventually lived to a ripe old age. Interestingly, the Old Courthouse had a recent visit from some of the living relatives of those accused of the crime and they added more information in support of the romantic version. They told us that when the coffin arrived in Fanad it was not taken directly into the main body of the church as normal but that it was carried instead into the sacristy. To let Heraghty out? The relatives also told us that after some time Heraghty's wife applied for permission to re-marry but was refused, leaving us with the assumption that her first husband was considered to be very much alive!

INSPECTOR MARTIN'S GHOST.

Another eerie account, also involving the clergy relates to the killing of Inspector Martin during the days of the Land League and the Gweedore evictions of the late 1880's. Although the incident did not take place in Lifford, it concerns the local leader of the movement, Father James McFadden, who spent some time here when he appeared at Lifford Courthouse where he was remanded for eight days. This story appeared in the first Donegal Annual of 1947.

"The most stirring event connected with Gweedore is the arrest of Father McFadden and the killing of Inspector Martin on Sunday the 3rd of February 1889. Father McFadden had championed the people's cause against the tyranny of the landlords. An order was given for his arrest but the civil authorities feared a tumult among the people. The priest's house was guarded by police. A night or two before the arrest, Constable Keenan was patrolling in front of the house when something happened that made him chill with terror. He averred that he saw in the moonlight, the form and face of Inspector Martin lying dead, adorned with

helmet and sword, but robed and shrouded as for the grave. He gazed at this form in wonder for a few moments. Then a cloud passed over the face of the moon and when the moon shone forth again the apparition had disappeared.

Martin very unwisely decided to arrest the priest on Sunday morning. Police surrounded the church and Martin, with seven men, took up position on the steps that led from the church to the residence of the priest.

After Mass, as Father McFadden was returning to his house, Inspector Martin intercepted him and said, 'I arrest you'. 'Produce your authority sir', said the priest. Thereupon the Inspector grabbed the priest's soutane by the collar rather roughly and at the same time brandished the sword which he held in his hand. The cry went through the people that the priest was being killed. The crowd rushed in and the Inspector, releasing his hold, tried to keep them back with his sword. Father McFadden was escorted to his house by two policemen, while the Inspector strove to ward off the angry crowd. In the ensuing confusion, Inspector Martin received a violent blow, and he fell to rise no more".

FOOTSTEPS IN THE NIGHT...

It is hardly surprising that an old building such as the Courthouse, with an atmosphere created by centuries of pain and suffering, should harbour the ghosts of the past. Even in the 20th century, some of the people who worked here could feel uncomfortable at times. Not so long ago, for instance, we had a visitor who told us that his father, Eddie Crawford, used to be a caretaker here and that many a scary incident had happened to him. Although Eddie is no longer with us, one of his friends gave us the story which follows:

"Eddie worked as caretaker with the Council for almost 40 years and was here all through the Second World War. At that time the Courthouse was heated by open turf fires and one of his jobs was to clean the chimneys. He was cleaning the chimney in the Grand Jury room upstairs on this particular dark, October night and he had a young fella in to make an extra couple of bob for himself. Eddie himself

was cleaning the chimney and the young fella's job was carrying out the soot. Anyway, Eddie said he was cleaning the chimney and the young fella had gone out with the bucket of soot and the next thing he thought he heard steps behind him. He didn't look round but he heard the door open and then these footsteps. When he did look round there was nobody there. After a bit the young fella came back with the empty bucket and he had another bucket ready for him and he said to him, `Make sure you close the door behind you on the way out' and he heard the door bang as the young fella left. After a bit he thought he heard the door opening again but he didn't pay much attention to it. When the young fella came up the stairs and in through the open door Eddie turned on him and said, `Look, I told you to close that door! There's an awful breeze and it's terribly cold.' The young fella said, `I did close it.' Eddie said, `You did not! Go and close it now.' So the young fella went down and closed the door and Eddie stood and watched him. He said the young fella came back and they stood watching the door, and the next thing it opened as gently as you like. He said had he not seen it he wouldn't have believed it. After that they didn't spend much longer cleaning the chimneys because the two of them ran out of it!! Now that was Eddie's story and he wasn't making it up. He didn't give me the name of the young fella because he was a local and he didn't want to embarrass him".

Detail of the front entrance to the Courthouse

THE SHERIFF AND THE SAILOR.

The Entrance Hall prior to renovations at the Courthouse

The balcony pictured above led on to the upstairs public gallery in the courtroom. It is believed that it was from this balcony that a daring escape was attempted in days gone by. This account was uncovered in an unsigned, undated newspaper article held in the County Archives in Lifford.

"I heard the old folks say that a female prisoner here (Lifford County Gaol) under sentence of death was set free under the following circumstances:

One morning, the Sheriff came to the prison to take charge of a sailor who was about to be guarded to the gallows for execution. The man managed to escape from the guards just at the door. He ran into the hall and up a ladder that stood there and through a trap-door to the top floor of the Courthouse. Soldiers were sent up after him but having picked up a piece of wood battered the head of each soldier as it appeared at the trap-door.

This warfare went on for some time, till at last the Sheriff went down amongst the prisoners and promised that if any of them volunteered to go up and hold the man above he would discharge him or her from gaol no matter what his or her crime was. This woman volunteered on the conditions named. She made the Sheriff get her two small creels, which she placed one upon the other, over her head, and with this novel helmet she ascended the ladder, reached the trap-door, withstood a furious assault, and eventually succeeded in getting through the trap-door, caught the man and kept her grip of

"...with this novel helmet she ascended the ladder..."

him until the soldiers followed her and put the shackles on the fugitive. He was taken down with some difficulty and hanged the same day. A week afterwards the woman was released".

A more successful escape appears to have taken place much earlier in the history of the Courthouse, only a few years after it was first opened. Unfortunately, we know little of the details except that it landed the Sub-Sheriff in hot water. This extract appeared in the Grand Jury Presentments for September 10th, 1759: *"£22 15s to John McCausland and James Nisbitt to reimburse them so much expended in persecuting and convicting Chris Armstrong, late Sub Sheriff, for misbehaviour in his office in neglecting and suffering William Barrett, a criminal tried and convicted in this County for cow stealing, for making his escape".*

Even more audacious was the jail-break in 1788 when seven prisoners absconded. How many were recaptured is unclear but this scale of break-out seems to have been rare.

The `New Gaol' built next to The Courthouse in 1793

THE LUNATIC ASYLUM

Over the years, the basement cell area of the Courthouse has been put to many uses including a lunatic asylum. Strangely enough, its origins as an institution for `imbeciles' and `idiots' is connected to the American War of Independence (1775-1783). After the colony broke away from British rule it refused to take any more convict labour. This caused a `confinement crisis' in Britain and Ireland and led to a massive gaol-building programme to cope with the number of prisoners who had been sentenced to transportation but had nowhere to go. When they began building the New Gaol next to the Courthouse in Lifford Diamond in 1793, it took the pressure off the small County Gaol which was then used as an asylum until the 1840's.

Containing up to 33 inmates at times, conditions in the early years of the 19th century were miserable, to say the least. In 1822, for instance, Dr Reid, a distinguished London physician, visited Ireland and subsequently published the result of his observations in a volume entitled *Travels in Ireland*. The following extract is based on his findings after his visit to the basement cells of the lunatic asylum in Lifford Courthouse:

"A place I shall always think on with horror. From its situation being partly underground, it is dark, unhealthy and everyway wretched. Although not quite unaccustomed to scenes of misery, the objects I beheld were quite appalling; the stench that issued from the dungeon walls of which are so prodigiously thick as to give a notion that the place was originally made bombproof, was so loathsome that, to use a vulgar but expressive phrase, `it would knock down a horse'".

When Dr.Reid visited the Asylum at Lifford, Mary Kelly had already spent four years there. Described as an `Incurable Maniac', she was to remain for another twenty-two years.

A modern day representation of what conditions were like for Mary Kelly in the Lunatic Asylum

THE UPS AND DOWNS OF LIFFORD COURTHOUSE

"Watch an old building with an anxious care, guard it as best you may, and at any cost from every influence of dilapidation. Count its stones as you would jewels of a crown; set watches about it as if at the gates of a besieged city; bind it together with iron where it loosens, stay it with timber where it declines; and do this tenderly, reverently and continually and many a generation will still be born and pass away beneath its shadows"
John Ruskin

The Courtroom prior to renovation

For fifty years, Ruskin's words went unheeded as far as Lifford Courthouse was concerned. Although it was *"one of the finest of the Ulster Sessions Houses built in the eighteenth century"*, after its last court case was heard in 1938 the building was allowed to fall into complete disrepair. In his book `Ulster Courthouses and Market Houses', C.E. Brett of the National Trust wrote in 1973: *"It is one of the finest buildings in the North and the most neglected. The interior of the Criminal Court has been gutted, even the ceiling has been removed, and the leaking slates propped up by two long telegraph poles, while the pigeons befoul the polling boxes stored there"*.

10 years later, things hadn't improved much when Frank McDonald of the *Irish Times* reported:

"The roof leaks badly, the interior walls are blotched by dampness, parts of the plaster cornice have fallen down and the large courtroom is just a shambles".

Lifford Courthouse before it was renovated

Thanks to the determination of some local people, who formed a committee dedicated to the regeneration of the area, this process was eventually reversed in the late 1980's. After further renovation, the Old Courthouse finally re-emerged in 1994 as an award-winning Heritage Centre attracting thousands of visitors each year.

However, it is not as if the building lay completely empty and unused for half a century. Far from it. Up until 1984, for instance, part of it was used as the central headquarters of Donegal County Libraries. After they moved, it reverted to Lifford Community Library which returned to the Courthouse recently after a spell on the Main Street. Other parts of the building were utilised by the County Council Land Registry, the Agricultural Committee and Donegal Archives Department while the dark, musty cells in the basement were used as a storage area by the roads department. Even the local children put it to their own use, with scallywags such the Sheils, the McIntyres and the Herrons treating it as their private playground.

But it was storage of another commodity that almost led to the complete destruction of this once impressive monument to the past. During the `Emergency' period of the Second World War, when coal was scarce, the building was converted into a Turf Depot which was then transported by rail to other `non-turf' producing areas such as Dublin. This situation continued for several years after the war until one night in May 1948 the turf in the Courthouse caught fire. Fortunately, the Strabane Fire Brigade managed to get to Lifford in time otherwise there would be no Courthouse today.

All in all, it has been quite a chequered career for the old building, but at least today its future is safe for a little while longer, especially if we keep John Ruskin's words in mind.

Lifford Courthouse as it stands today

BIBLIOGRAPHY

NEWSPAPERS, PERIODICALS AND MANUSCRIPTS

Strabane Morning Post
Derry Journal
Strabane/Lifford Notes
The Old Courthouse News
Donegal Annual
The Rupert Coughlan Collection
Irish Statutes 1785-1786 Vol xiii, pp776-778
County Donegal Grand Jury Presentments
Report by Rev. John Graham to the North West Society. 8th October, 1821
Lifford Courthouse Research Papers
The Works of Michael Priestley both Known and Attributed. BSc Dissertation. Malachy McGarrigle. 1988
Interview with Leo Friel. Billy Patton, Sept. 2003

PUBLICATIONS

Mountjoy. The Story of a Prison. Tim Carey. Collins Press. 2000
A History of Kilmainham Gaol. Freida Kelly. Mercier Press. 1988
The Hanging Tree. V.A.C. Gatrell. Oxford University Press. 1994
The Women of Botany Bay. Portia Robinson. Macquarie Library. 1988
Australia – The Early Years. Brian Mitchell (ed). Genealogy Centre, Derry.
Half-Hanged MacNaghten. Darrinagh Boyle. Guildhall Press. 1993
The Fair River Valley. Jim Bradley et al. Ulster Historical Foundation. 2000
By the Banks of the Mourne. Michael Kennedy. Strabane. 1996
Emigrants from Ireland to America, 1735-1743. Transcription of the Report of the Irish House of Commons into enforced emigration to America. Francis McDonnell